The Animal School

The Administration of the School Curriculum
with References to Individual Differences

by George H. Reavis

With a Foreword and Epilogue
by
Char Forsten, Jim Grant, and Irv Richardson

Illustrations by
Joyce Orchard Garamella

Crystal Springs
BOOKS

Published by
Crystal Springs Books • Peterborough, New Hampshire
1-800-321-0401

The Animal School: The Administration of the School Curriculum
with References to Individual Differences
by George H. Reavis
Illustrated by Joyce Orchard Garamella
Illustrations © 1999 Crystal Springs Books
Design by Susan Dunholter
All rights reserved. Printed in the United States of America.
Published by Crystal Springs Books, 10 Sharon Road, PO Box 500, Peterborough, NH 03458.
Phone 1-800-321-0401

09 08 07 06 05   3 4 5 6 7

ISBN 1-884548-31-8

DEDICATION

Dedicated to those children and adults who have unjustly suffered the fate
of standardized tests and inappropriate curriculum and standards.

Char Forsten   Jim Grant   Sw Richardson

FOREWORD

In the early 1940s, George H. Reavis, then assistant superintendent of Cincinnati Public Schools, wrote a call to action. He called it *The Animal School*. Originally written for the *Public School Bulletin*, *The Animal School* has become a timeless and, as the reader will discover, timely allegory about the dangers inherent in blind reform policies.

Our message to you: Believe that children learn best when we, their teachers, develop and challenge their strengths and identify and nurture their weaknesses.

Take action.

Once upon a time . . .

The animals decided they must do something
heroic to meet the problems of a " new world."

So they organized a school.

They adopted an activity curriculum consisting of running, climbing, swimming, and flying.

To make it easier to administer the curriculum,
all the animals took all the subjects.

The duck was excellent in swimming —
in fact, better than his instructor.

But he made only passing grades in flying
and was very poor in running.

Since he was slow in running,
he had to stay after school and also drop
swimming in order to practice running.

This was kept up until his webbed feet were badly
worn and he was only average in swimming.
But average was acceptable in school, so nobody
worried about that except the duck.

The rabbit started at the top of the class in running but had a nervous breakdown because

of so much make-up work in swimming.

The squirrel was excellent in climbing until he
developed frustration in the flying class, where
his teacher made him start from the ground up
instead of the treetop down.

He also developed a charley horse from overexertion and then got a C in climbing and a D in running.

The eagle was a problem child and was
disciplined severely.

In the climbing class he beat all the others to the top of the tree but insisted on using his own way to get there.

At the end of the year, an abnormal eel that could swim exceedingly well, and also run, climb, and fly a little, had the highest average,

and he was valedictorian.

The prairie dogs stayed out of school and fought the tax levy because the administration would not add digging and burrowing to the curriculum.

They apprenticed their children to a badger
and later joined the ground hogs and gophers
to start a successful private school.

Does this fable have a moral?

Epilogue

As educators, we spend our entire careers affirming the fact that each student is a unique and individual learner. Mandatory assessments, achievement-test scores, and IQ screenings confirm this knowledge. We document, read about, attend conferences on, teach to, and publicly acknowledge these very differences. But to what end? Despite indisputable results, many districts continue to mandate that educators teach the same curriculum in the same way to all students, regardless of ability.
Thankfully, current brain research, foremost including Howard Gardner's Multiple Intelligence Theory, is opening doors ever wider to our understanding of how we learn.

George H. Reavis believed, as do we and thousands of educators around the country believe today, that solutions to our education dilemmas can and must be found.
We believe that public funds should be used to make our schools places where children are held to high, yet different, standards, because" covering the curriculum" won't advance us far as a society if we fail to recognize each child as an individual learner.
Remember: There is no one correct way to teach all children,
but there is a correct way to teach each child: one at a time. If you know a policy maker, share with him or her a copy of this book.

U.S. Cataloging-in-Publication Data
   (Library of Congress Standards)

Reavis, George H.(George Harve) b. 1883.
          The animal school : the administration of the school
curriculum with references to individual differences / by
George H. Reavis : with a foreword and epilogue by
Char Forsten, Jim Grant and Irv Richardson ; illustrations by
Joyce Orchard Garamella.-1st. ed.
[24] p. : col. Ill. : cm.
Reprint: Cincinnati, Ohio: Cincinnati Public School Bulletin,
1940?
Summary : Fable in which animals illustrate the dangers of
students being forced to conform to developmentally
inappropriate practices.
ISBN 1-884548-31-8
1. Learning-Study and teaching. 2. Teaching-Addresses,
essays, lectures. 3. Curriculum planning. . I. Garamella,
Joyce Orchard, 1952-. II. Title.
371.2 -dc21 1999 CIP